Marie Durand

by Simonetta Carr

with Illustrations by Matt Abraxas

REFORMATION HERITAGE BOOKS

Grand Rapids, Michigan

Marie Durand
© 2015 by Simonetta Carr

Cover artwork by Matt Abraxas: Marie wrote letters in the name of all the prisoners.

For additional artwork by Matt, see pages 9, 13, 15, 17, 21, 31, 33, 35, 41, 43, 47, and 49.

Reformation Heritage Books
2965 Leonard St. NE
Grand Rapids, MI 49525
616-977-0889
e-mail: orders@heritagebooks.org
website: www.heritagebooks.org

Printed in the United States of America
21 22 23 24 25 26/10 9 8 7 6 5 4 3 2

Library of Congress Cataloging-in-Publication Data

Carr, Simonetta, author.
  Marie Durand / by Simonetta Carr ; with illustrations by Matt Abraxas.
    pages cm. — (Christian biographies for young readers)
  ISBN 978-1-60178-390-5 (hardcover : alk. paper)
1. Durand, Marie, 1715-1776—Juvenile literature. 2. Huguenots—Biography—Juvenile literature. 3. Dissenters, Religious—Biography—Juvenile literature. 4. Religious minorities—France—History—Juvenile literature. 5. France—Church history—18th century—Juvenile literature. I. Abraxas, Matt, illustrator. II. Title.
  BX9459.D83C37 2015
  284.5092—dc23
                          2015013747

For additional Reformed literature, request a free book list from Reformation Heritage Books at the above address.

CHRISTIAN BIOGRAPHIES FOR YOUNG READERS

This series introduces children to important people in the Christian tradition. Parents and schoolteachers alike will welcome the excellent educational value it provides for students, while the quality of the publication and the artwork make each volume a keepsake for generations to come. Furthermore, the books in the series go beyond the simple story of someone's life by teaching young readers the historical and theological relevance of each character.

AVAILABLE VOLUMES OF THE SERIES

John Calvin
Augustine of Hippo
John Owen
Athanasius
Lady Jane Grey
Anselm of
   Canterbury
John Knox
Jonathan Edwards
Marie Durand

Martin Luther
Peter Martyr
   Vermigli
Irenaeus of Lyon
John Newton
Julia Gonzaga
B.B. Warfield
John Bunyan
Phillis Wheatley

Table of Contents

MAP CREATED BY TOM CARROLL

N
W
S
PARIS
FRANCE
SWITZERLAND
LAUSANNE
GENEVA
MASSIF CENTRAL
LYON
Bouschet de Pranles
Privas
Rhône River
Cévennes
Nimes
Montpellier
Aigues-Mortes
Fort Brescou

A map of France and Switzerland during Marie's life

Introduction

Born in the enchanting region between the Rhone River and the Massif Central mountains in Southern France, Marie Durand chose to spend most of her life in a dark, unhealthy prison rather than follow a religion she considered contrary to the teachings of Christ.

Life had not always been so difficult for French Protestants such as Marie. In 1598, a little more than one hundred years before Marie's birth, King Henry IV, who had become Roman Catholic, made an unusual decision. At that time, most kings required their subjects to follow their religion. But to put an end to decades of religious wars, Henry passed a law allowing Protestants to live in France according to their conscience.

GILLES DESPINS, HTTP://WWW.TOURDECONSTANCE.COM/MARIEDURAND/, PUBLISHED WITH PERMISSION

We don't have any pictures of Marie Durand, so we don't know what she looked like. This is a reconstruction of what might have been her bedroom in her house in Bouschet de Pranles, France.

NATIONAL GALLERY OF ART, GIFT OF MISS ELLEN T. BULLARD

Louis XIV

Because of this law, called the Edict of Nantes, Protestants enjoyed greater peace. Not everyone in France, however, agreed with the king. Some were afraid Protestants would become so strong that they could take over the country. Many thought it would be easier to have just one religion for all. Gradually, the new kings of France returned to the old habits, depriving Protestants of their rights.

In 1685, Henry's grandson, King Louis XIV, officially revoked the law that protected Protestants. Under his rules, about seven hundred Protestant churches were destroyed. All pastors were banned from the country and had to leave their properties behind. If they had children over the age of seven, they had to leave them in France with Roman Catholic families and pay for their room and board. Most pastors went to Switzerland, Germany, Holland, or England. Some sailed to North America. A few stayed in France and continued to hold secret meetings.

For all other Protestants, the situation became even more difficult because they were not allowed to leave France. Instead, the government sent special soldiers called Dragoons to Protestant families to force them to turn to the Roman Catholic Church. Meeting for public worship according to the Protestant faith became dangerous. If caught, the men were sentenced to forced work on warships called galleys, and the women were sent to prison. Only those who lived near the border or had enough financial means were able to secretly flee.

In 1702, after years of abuses, some Protestants started a war of rebellion and self-defense against the government. They were known as Camisards because they wore white shirts (*camisa* means "shirt" in the language of a certain French region) so they could recognize each other at night.

The Camisards were few in comparison with the king's troops, but they knew the mountainous area much better and were ready to die for their freedom. To fight back, Roman Catholic authorities formed their own group of revolutionary fighters. The war caused many losses on both sides. It ended in 1704, but uprisings continued until 1710, after the Camisards' main leaders had died.

CHAPTER ONE
Outlaw from Birth

The Durands' home

By July 15, 1711, when Marie Durand let out her first cry in a small stone house at Bouschet de Pranles, a tiny French village, the wars had quieted down. Her parents, Étienne and Claudine, were probably relieved. To live in peace, they had made some compromises, allowing the children to be baptized in the Roman Catholic Church. Their first son, Pierre, who was eleven when Marie was born, had been receiving Roman Catholic instruction in the local school. At home, however, Étienne and Claudine taught their children the Protestant faith they had learned from their parents.

Since Protestant teachings were illegal, they built a hiding place inside a wall where they kept their Bible, their Protestant catechism, a psalter (a book of the Psalms put to music), and other Christian books. They also had a hiding place near the sheep barn where they could run in case of danger or give hospitality to preachers who passed through their town.

At home, Étienne and Claudine taught their children the Protestant faith they had learned from their parents.

Around the house, Marie and her family had frequent reminders of God's love and care. Two inscriptions especially stood before their eyes. The first was in Latin. Étienne had engraved it on the front door of their house almost ten years after the Revocation of the Edict of Nantes: "Have mercy on me, Lord God." The second, engraved two years later over the fireplace, was in French. It was a message of gratefulness: "God be praised!"

Being one of the few townspeople who had a formal education, Étienne worked as the town's clerk, taking care of most records, except for baptisms, marriages, and deaths, which by law had to be recorded by a priest. Like most people in that region, he also had a small farm that produced enough food for the family's needs. Claudine cared for the house, the garden, the animals, and the crops. After finishing his basic studies, Pierre started to work for a notary in the nearby town of Privas, issuing documents like his father. Most likely, Marie attended the local school because her letters show she learned to write better than her father.

Engraving on the Durands' fireplace

CHAPTER TWO
A Family Divided

In 1715, when Marie was only four, King Louis XIV died. France was then run by one of Louis's relatives until his great-grandson (his only heir) came of legal age. Taking advantage of this time of change, some pastors met secretly to discuss the future and unity of the French churches. Pierre became involved. While working in Privas, he had come to know some of these pastors, and they had encouraged him to become a pastor too.

Soon French Protestants started to gather more frequently for worship. In January 1719, the Durands joined others for worship at a private home belonging to Claudine. This time of worship and hearing the gospel was so inspiring that everyone agreed to meet again in the evening, this time in the woods. Between services, Pierre Durand and his best friend Pierre Rouvier went around the area inviting others. They didn't know, however, that the morning service had been attended by a spy who had informed the authorities.

GILLES DESPINS, HTTP://WWW.TOUR DECONSTANCE.COM/MARIEDURAND/, PUBLISHED WITH PERMISSION

The Cave of Fairies, near the area where Marie was born, was used for Protestant meetings.

11

The evening service had just started when soldiers attacked the place, capturing three girls and shooting at those who were fleeing. The night was dark, so most people, including Pierre and his friend, managed to escape. Three months later, some guards returned to the area, destroyed the house where the meeting had taken place, and arrested Claudine because she was the owner of the house.

Some of the guards stayed at the Durands' home for twenty-one days, hoping that Pierre would return. Finally they left, taking with them some of Étienne's animals and furniture. Étienne received news of Claudine seven years later, after she had already died.

Claudine's arrest must have been a painful experience for Marie, who was then seven years old. Undoubtedly, her father helped her understand what the Bible teaches about God's providence and care for His children in their trials.

The evening church service had just started when soldiers attacked the place of worship.

As for Pierre, seven months after the raid he wrote a loving letter to his parents, explaining he had decided to become a pastor and preach the gospel in spite of the dangers. To reach this goal, he was attending a school in Switzerland.

He returned home at least once, but briefly and in private. Étienne and Marie must have treasured every minute with him, listening to stories of his travels, his preaching in secret, and his work with other pastors in the reorganization of the church.

The reorganization was much needed. Most of the trained pastors had been forced to leave France, so for years many had been preaching without any training. Others, even children, had been giving messages they claimed to have received directly from God. Like many pastors, Pierre thought this type of "prophecy" was more dangerous than persecution, because anyone can claim his words are a message from God. This can distract from studying the Bible and bring disunity, deceit, and confusion.

Marie must have treasured every moment with Pierre when he returned home, briefly and in secret.

In 1726, Pierre was officially ordained minister of God's Word. Around the same time, he became engaged to a young woman named Anne Rouvier, a sister of his best friend. Étienne must have been both excited and fearful. What kind of life could Pierre, an outlaw, offer his wife and children, especially after King Louis XV, who had come of age, had ordered that all Protestant preachers must die?

Louis XV

Two years later, the danger came close to home. One day at dawn, a troop of soldiers headed for Étienne's house. Because he was the father of a wanted man, Étienne ran to a nearby castle, probably leaving seventeen-year-old Marie with some neighbors. After searching every corner of the house, the soldiers found the family's Bible, psalter, and other books, including Étienne's diary, and took them as proof of the Durands' transgression.

A band of soldiers searched every corner of Marie's house.

One month later, Étienne, still in hiding, was discovered and taken to the local authorities, who threatened to put him in a "prison where he would be bound for the rest of his days." As a way out, they told him "to work with all his might to make sure his son left the kingdom."

Afraid for both himself and his son, Étienne wrote Pierre, "Have mercy on me once, considering my age and the grief I am suffering, and also take care of yourself."

Pierre had a difficult decision to make. Should he leave the country and stop preaching the gospel to his people? Or should he stay and put his father at greater risk? Finally, he realized he had to obey his calling. Besides, he didn't trust the government's promises. He wasn't sure they wouldn't still capture him at the border and keep his father in prison anyway.

In the end, Pierre wrote a letter to the king's commander, saying, "Suppose, for a time, I am a criminal, as you think. Please allow me to ask you, sir, if the king orders you to punish a father for the alleged crimes of his son? Is it possible to believe that this is done in the states of a prince who has the great glory of wearing the august title of Most Christian?" Pierre explained that even if they thought their actions were right, he could not obey their orders because God wanted him to continue to pastor the people He had entrusted to his care.

TELLINE DE MER

Fort Brescou

After receiving Pierre's reply, the authorities sent Étienne to the prison at Fort Brescou, on a small island of the Mediterranean Sea. Marie remained at home alone, with her animals and her fields.

INGO MEHLING, WIKIMEDIA COMMONS

The Tower of Constance

It was around that time that Mathieu Serre asked for Marie's hand in marriage. He was at least ten years older than she was and might have been a friend of the family. Marie wrote her father to ask for his advice, but she never received his reply. Since the decision rested on her, she finally agreed to marry Mathieu, even though Pierre, when he heard about it, disapproved of her choice.

Marie's hopes for a future as bride and mother didn't last long, however, as she and Mathieu were arrested together simply because she was the sister of a Protestant pastor. Mathieu was sent to Fort Brescou, and Marie to the Tower of Constance, an ancient building that had been used as a watchtower and prison. The city around the Tower, Aigues-Mortes, had originally been a seaport. Over time, the sea had receded, and the area had turned into a swamp full of disease-carrying mosquitoes.

Marie was taken prisoner to the Tower of Constance.

CHAPTER THREE
The Tower

LACHLAN MCFETRIDGE, FLICKR.

The ceiling of the Tower, with a central hole

In the Tower, Marie found about twenty-five other women prisoners with a few children and two small babies. She knew at least some by name. Most of them had been arrested at worship meetings. Some were imprisoned because they had married with a Protestant ceremony.

The prisoners spent their days together in a large room. When it rained, water entered freely through both a large grated hole in the ceiling and the narrow openings in the walls that served as windows, so the place was either flooded or very humid. Even the firewood used for heating or cooking was often wet, filling the room with a thick smoke as it burned. The same openings allowed snow to enter in the winter and hot air and mosquitoes in the summer. On some occasions the prisoners were allowed to go on the terrace, a flat, open place at the top of the tower, to get some fresh air.

Days went by slowly. At night the prisoners slept on benches covered with straw. Each had a sheet and a blanket. Their daily diet was composed of water and a pound and a half of bread per person. Sometimes friends sent extra food—mostly rice, beans, lard, and chestnuts—which the women cooked in the fireplace. Every day the women prayed and sang together using a psalter.

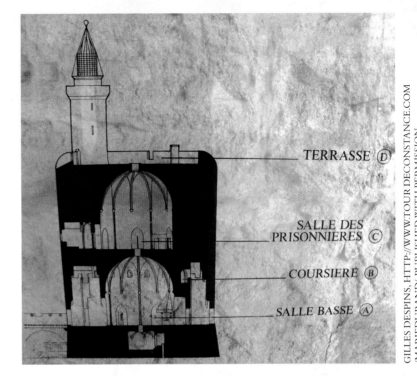

A plan of the Tower. A = lower hall;
B = passageway; C = prisoners' hall; D = terrace

Whenever someone sent some cotton yarn or pieces of cloth and some thread, the prisoners made or repaired their clothes. Sometimes they made embroideries for the guards' wives to thank them for their kindness. Otherwise, there was still plenty to do caring for the babies, the elderly, and the sick. Occasionally the guards asked the women to do work for them and paid them with a little money or food.

The prisoners always had time to talk, telling stories of past lives, sharing letters and news, and discussing their hopes of freedom and encouraging each other with God's Word. Visitors were allowed, but were rare.

Usually the women got along well, but when many people are crowded in one room, it's easy to have disagreements. The women had to accept difficult personalities, understand occasional mood swings, and forgive each other. Once, when bickering became particularly frequent, Antoine Court, one of the main pastors of the newly reformed church, wrote a letter to remind the women of the privilege of suffering for Christ and the importance of peace.

Since some of the women had called themselves prophetesses before they were arrested, he reminded them to cling to the Bible as God's only sure Word. "Stop running after the fantasies you so often followed," he wrote. "Only the Word of God can make you wise to learn and succeed in every good work."

The common prison room in the Tower of Constance

DAVID QUICK

Marie must have been eager to receive news from her family. Only two months after her arrest, Étienne wrote her a comforting letter telling her not to grieve, but "to rejoice always and in every moment in the Lord with prayers, psalms, and hymns." The Lord would use these things to give Marie the strength to bear all her afflictions, Étienne said. Mathieu, who shared the same cell with Étienne, added a few lines to express the pain of his separation from Marie—a pain so excruciating that he had not been able to eat or drink until Étienne gave him comfort. "I beg you, my dear darling," Mathieu wrote her, "to believe as if faith was your bread." Sadly, the letter was intercepted, and Marie was never able to read it.

KAROLY LORENTEY

A bedroom at Fort Brescou.
Étienne and Mathieu shared the same bed.

The following year, she finally received some news—but from an unexpected source. Isabelle Rouvier, Pierre's mother-in-law, entered the Tower as a prisoner in spite of her protests that she had nothing to do with her son-in-law's pastoral ministry. In fact, she had always been against his marriage with her daughter and had been trying to persuade the authorities to annul it since it was not performed in the Roman Catholic Church.

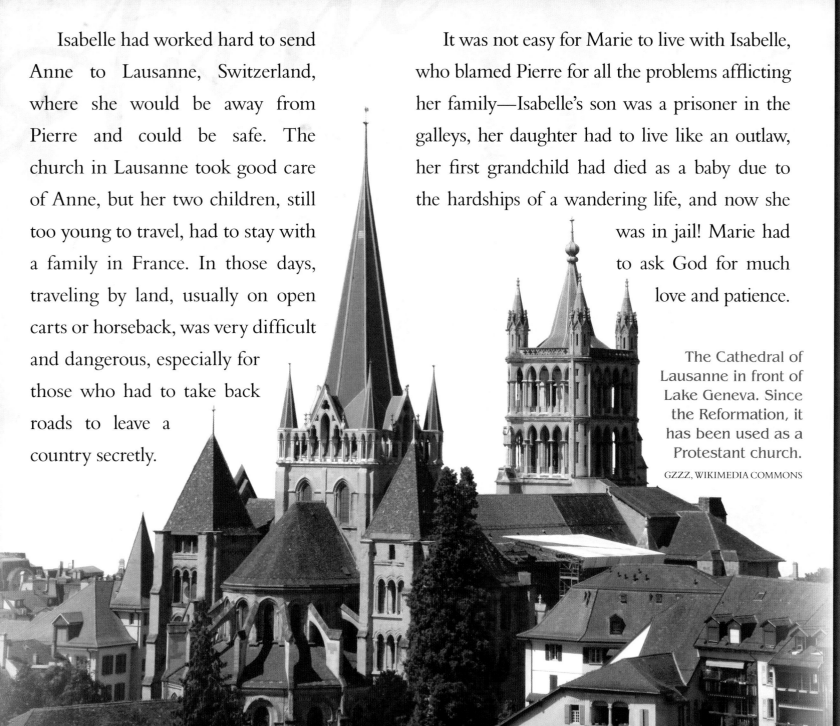

Isabelle had worked hard to send Anne to Lausanne, Switzerland, where she would be away from Pierre and could be safe. The church in Lausanne took good care of Anne, but her two children, still too young to travel, had to stay with a family in France. In those days, traveling by land, usually on open carts or horseback, was very difficult and dangerous, especially for those who had to take back roads to leave a country secretly.

It was not easy for Marie to live with Isabelle, who blamed Pierre for all the problems afflicting her family—Isabelle's son was a prisoner in the galleys, her daughter had to live like an outlaw, her first grandchild had died as a baby due to the hardships of a wandering life, and now she was in jail! Marie had to ask God for much love and patience.

The Cathedral of Lausanne in front of Lake Geneva. Since the Reformation, it has been used as a Protestant church.

GZZZ, WIKIMEDIA COMMONS

The city of Aigues-Mortes around the Tower of Constance

In the end, it seems Isabelle was able to submit at least in part to God's will. We know this from a letter Pierre wrote to Anne to encourage her to look to God, who had prevented her mother from doing them harm. "Thank God, her conscience has awakened," he said. "She knows she did wrong, if what they have told me is true." In any case, Isabelle never took the easy way out of jail—she never denied her Protestant faith.

Isabelle probably gave Marie some news about Anne and the children. They were all safe, but Anne was often lonely and worried about her family. As for Pierre, he was still—after nearly thirteen years—traveling secretly around France, preaching the gospel and baptizing believers and their children. In his letters to Anne, he kept assuring her of his desire to bring the family together.

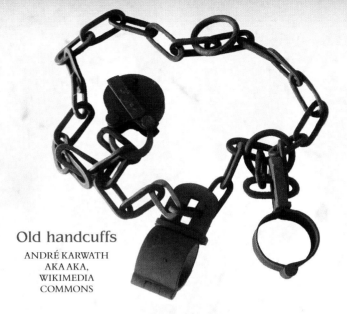

Old handcuffs
ANDRÉ KARWATH
AKA AKA,
WIKIMEDIA
COMMONS

In the meantime, since the government's attempts to capture Pierre by punishing the members of his family had failed, the authorities promised an extremely high reward to anyone who would reveal his location. This plan worked.

On February 12, 1732, as Pierre was visiting some friends, he was spotted by a woman who reported him to the authorities. Without wasting time, the captain appointed a band of soldiers to wait for him on the road he was going to take.

Unaware of this trap, Pierre had dinner with his friends, then stayed a little longer to help them shell some nuts. He left around ten o'clock, exactly when the soldiers were leaving to reach their hiding place.

Eighteenth-century French pistol
RAMA, WIKIMEDIA COMMONS

Pierre rode alone, in spite of his friends' offer to ride with him. The region was covered by a thick forest of birch and chestnut trees, hiding the soldiers from his sight. When the guards suddenly appeared, he instinctively reached for the gun he carried to protect himself from wolves and robbers. As soon as he realized they were guards, he pulled his hand back. Just as the other pastors of the newly reformed church, he believed the Bible teaches us not to fight the authorities God has appointed.

The soldiers led Pierre to their superiors, who questioned him with the help of a priest. Finally, they escorted him to a prison to prepare for his execution. As he rode through a large crowd that had gathered to see him, he sang the words of Psalm 25, "Unto thee, O LORD, do I lift up my soul."

On the day of his execution, he begged the authorities to release his relatives from prison since there was no need to keep them there. Then he went to his death singing more psalms. Soon after his death, his children reunited with their mother. Étienne, Mathieu, Marie, and Isabelle remained in prison.

When the guards suddenly appeared, Pierre instinctively reached for the gun
he carried to protect himself from wolves and robbers.

CHAPTER FOUR
Leader and Friend

In the Tower, Marie gradually assumed the role of a leader. Since only one-third of the prisoners could read and write, and even fewer could do so well, she often led the time of daily devotions and wrote letters in the name of all, asking for help and supplies and thanking

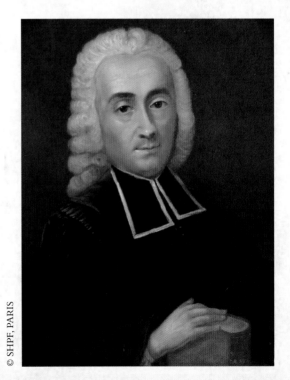

© SHPF, PARIS

Paul Rabaut

those who gave. Their main supporters were Paul Rabaut, an influential French pastor, and the French-speaking church in Amsterdam, Holland. Over time, other people learned about the prisoners' conditions and were moved to help.

There were, however, long periods of time when it seemed as though the whole world had forgotten these women, and Marie had to encourage other believers to remember their duty of charity toward those who are in prison. "The Lord Jesus promises to reward when a glass of cold water is given to His children. Even more so He will reward those who provide welcome sustenance to His elect who fight under the banner of the cross," she wrote.

Marie wrote letters in the name of all the prisoners.

Because of her knowledge and skills, Marie taught other prisoners' children both the Scriptures and the basic school subjects. She must have remembered many of the lessons her parents taught her when she was a child. The children loved her. In one of her letters, she talks about a young girl who often jumped up to hug and kiss her.

The mother of one of the children, Isabeau Menet, became one of Marie's closest friends. Isabeau and Marie were about the same age, shared the same deep love for God and the Scriptures, and loved to write. They often encouraged each other to be faithful to God until death, remembering that whatever God calls us to do is, in Isabeau's words, "for His glory and our salvation."

HUYGENS! AKA GSATIFAN/FLICKR.COM

A window in the tower

Marie taught the children of other prisoners both the Scriptures and the basic school subjects.

Sadly, a few years after her imprisonment, Isabeau received news that her husband, who had been captured with her during an outdoor church service and had been sent to the galleys, was dead. Isabeau mourned deeply.

Soon after that, another pain struck Isabeau's heart. The government determined that her son was too old to stay in a women's prison and should be sent to some relatives. While she trusted in God's providence, the separation from her son was so difficult that she became afflicted with a mental illness. By the time the authorities sent her back to her family, her mind was unable to function well. She had been in the Tower for about fifteen years.

Seeing her friend suffer so intensely must have been very difficult for Marie. She probably clung to the same promises she and Isabeau used to recite together, knowing "that the sufferings of this present time are not worthy to be compared with the glory which shall be revealed in us" (Romans 8:18).

CHAPTER FIVE
Resisting

GILLES DESPINS, HTTP://WWW.TOURDECONSTANCE.COM/MARIEDURAND/, PUBLISHED WITH PERMISSION

This small room was directly in front of the entrance to the prisoners' hall. The prisoners who were desperate to leave the Tower were brought there to sign a letter that said they officially denied their Protestant faith.

Some of the saddest occasions were the times when other prisoners left their Protestant faith in exchange for their freedom. It was a strong temptation. To be free from that dark and unhealthy place, a prisoner had to declare she believed in the Roman Catholic Church and prove it by attending Mass for some time. The priest and the Tower's supervisor felt very sorry for the women but couldn't help them unless they renounced their Protestant faith. It was hard for the other prisoners to watch the few who made this difficult decision.

Once, the Tower's supervisor gave the women an even easier choice. He suggested they write the king to say that they had attended Protestant worship because they thought he allowed it, and then ask for his forgiveness. It was true enough because the women respected the king and sincerely wondered if he was aware of those cruel laws. Still, it was an admission of guilt and a declaration that the king had the right to decide how God should be worshiped. The women could not accept the offer. Only one woman did, but she died three days before her freedom was granted.

ELIZABETH ISAKSON

It might have been during one of those times that a prisoner—many think it was Marie—engraved a word in a stone ledge in the middle of the common room: *Register,* which means "to resist" in the language of that particular region.

The word *Register* on the stone ledge

To resist became harder with time as the prisoners aged and illnesses became more painful and more frequent. Isabelle Rouvier became paralyzed and had to depend on the help of the other women—especially Marie—for nine years until she died.

Marie was frequently sick. It might have been malaria, a disease carried by mosquitoes that causes recurring high fevers. She also had rheumatism, a painful and persistent illness often caused by a cold and humid climate. "This year I felt its sharpness," she wrote to her niece, Anne, "especially in my head. I cried for a week. I felt I was dying every moment. It was in the cold weather, and our prisons were overflowing water everywhere, and I could find no cure; but now I'm better, thanks to the Lord."

Marie's correspondence with her niece was one of the sweetest comforts she had during her imprisonment. She loved Anne like a daughter and wrote her frequently. Her correspondence became even more frequent after Anne's mother, who had been sick for many years, died. Often, when Marie had some cloth or yarn, she deprived herself of new clothes to make some for the young girl. Most of all, she encouraged Anne to stay strong in the faith her parents had taught her.

Marc Antoine René de Voyer de Paulmy,
Marquis d'Argenson

Most likely, Marie continued to send letters to her father, even though there are none left today. She must have been overjoyed in 1743 when he was released from prison and was able to return home, where he lived to the age of ninety-two. Seven years later, Mathieu was also released, but the authorities ordered him to leave France forever, and Marie never saw him again. News of freed prisoners filled the women with hope. Perhaps soon it would be their turn.

Hopes mounted in 1750 when, after a meeting with Paul Rabaut and a letter from the women, a government officer, the Marquis of Paulmy d'Argenson, visited the Tower. The pitiful state of the women touched him so deeply that he gave each some money and asked them to pray for him. When two young girls fell at his feet crying, asking him to free their mothers, the marquis could hardly hold back his tears, and he promised to remember their request.

When the women at the Tower fell at his feet crying, the Marquis of Paulmy could hardly hold back his tears.

The marquis's good intentions could not do much to change the authorities' minds. Still, the idea that banning a religion is wrong was becoming more common, and many influential people wrote books to prove this point. Because of this, Paul Rabaut, still an outlaw, was able to safely meet some officials and explain the sufferings of French Protestants. In the fall of 1755, more prisoners were freed. "The chains of our captives begin to fall," Rabaut wrote. "It is hoped that gradually they will all be released."

Marie shared similar words of hope with her niece: "My dear angel, do not grieve. The time seems long and, indeed, it is, because we are naturally impatient, our flesh still complains, but my dear daughter, let's put to death our evil desires…. We will have the sweet satisfaction of meeting and embracing each other."

While she waited on God's deliverance, Marie tried to arrange a visit from Anne. The project occupied her time as she raised money and gave Anne some ideas. Finally, in 1759, Anne moved to France and was able to spend a whole month in Aigues-Mortes, paying several visits to her aunt. It was the happiest time Marie had experienced since her imprisonment.

Anne's visit was the happiest time Marie had experienced since her imprisonment.

CHAPTER SIX
Free at Last

As time progressed, French authorities became more tolerant toward other religions. By 1760, most of the persecution against Protestants stopped. Even so, few people in France knew there were still some Protestants working as slaves in the galleys or suffering in the Tower. Marie continued to write influential people and encouraged Rabaut to write the king.

"We are surrounded by darkness, smoke choking us," she wrote to a prominent lady at the royal court. "It is the horror of horrors, we could say early hell…in order to follow the divine principles of a religion which commands us to render unto Caesar what belongs to Caesar and to God what is God's."

Once in a while, the prisoners received news that their liberation had been granted. Then nothing happened. This seesaw of good news and disappointments was so discouraging that it affected their health.

It was only in 1766 that the Prince de Beauvau, who had served for almost twenty years as military commander of the region, learned about the prisoners in the Tower. Immediately he sent a petition to Louis Phélypeaux de Saint-Florentin, the official "Minister for the so-called Reformed religion." In spite of being one of the most unwavering enemies of French Protestants, the minister agreed to release two of the oldest women if they could produce some form of repentance.

Instead of simply forwarding the orders to the Tower, the Prince of Beauvau decided to visit the prisoners in person. Deeply moved by what he saw, he released two women immediately, without following the minister's procedure. Later, he continued to press the government for the release of the others. Marie must have made a strong impression on him because she was first on his list. Slowly, the government started to act.

Charles-Just, prince de Beauvau-Craon
by Elise Bruyere

Louis Phélypeaux de Saint-Florentin
by Louis Michel van Loo

On April 14, 1768, after thirty-eight years in prison, Marie was released, together with her friend Marie Vey-Goutète. She was fifty-seven years old, and her friend a little older. By December 15, 1768, only five women were still in the Tower. Still unsatisfied, the prince released the others on his own initiative. After the prisoners left, he had the prison locked up "in the hope that it would never again be opened for such a purpose."

Furious, the minister called him to be tried in court for insubordination, ordering that he must recapture the women or lose his position. The prince replied that while the minister certainly had the power to fire his subordinates, he could not stop them from acting according to their conscience and honor.

Marie was released from prison after thirty-eight years.

GILLES DESPINS, HTTP://WWW.TOURDECONSTANCE.COM /MARIEDURAND/, PUBLISHED WITH PERMISSION

The side door of Marie's home

In the meantime, Marie returned to her house in Bouschet de Pranles, where she lived with Marie Vey-Goutète. Together, the two women went back to the same life Marie remembered as a child—growing vegetables, cooking soup, roasting chestnuts, keeping the fire going, and fetching water. They continued to read the Bible, pray, and sing psalms together.

Marie's troubles, however, were not completely over. After her father's death, some cousins had taken over her farm, using the fields and robbing the house of many items, including the floorboards. Because Marie had not been able to inherit the house legally while she was in prison, she had to pay her cousins a lot of money to get her property back.

Marie and her friend Marie Vey-Goutète continued to read the Bible, pray, and sing psalms together.

There was an additional sadness. Anne, her niece, had married a rich Roman Catholic man and had stopped corresponding with her. In fact, instead of supporting her needy aunt, Anne had allowed her husband to rent out part of Marie's farm without asking for her permission and to charge Marie for any repairs he had to make.

Life in prison had weakened Marie's body and damaged her health. Working was difficult. Even if she mortgaged her property, she had no way of raising all the necessary money without relying on the goodness of the church. Once again she wrote Paul Rabaut, who in turn convinced the French church in Amsterdam to support her with a yearly donation. Moved by their generosity, Marie wrote, "What do I owe you, gentlemen? I owe you my life!"

Marie continued to rely on God's providence until the end of her life and died peacefully in her home at the age of sixty-five.

Marie's dining room

Epilogue

About eleven years after Marie's death, France passed a law recognizing Protestant baptisms and marriages. Two years later, as a result of the French Revolution, Protestants were able to worship freely. Some of the greatest promoters of this freedom of religion, however, were philosophers (students of the meaning and nature of life) who disagreed with much of the Bible. To them, living well and accepting each other was much more important than understanding what the Bible said.

A commemorative stone in memory of the persecuted Huguenots (French Protestants). The cross on top is the Huguenots' symbol. The dove represents the Holy Spirit. The grid represents the prison, and the galley is one of the warships where Protestant men were sentenced to forced labor for life.

Soon, instead of keeping both an important respect for others' beliefs and their own convictions about the life, death, and resurrection of Christ, many Protestants—including the sons of Paul Rabaut and Antoine Court—started to follow these philosophers' teachings. During that Age of Reason, or Enlightenment, as that time became known, they started to reject or ignore most teachings human beings can't fully explain, such as that God works miracles, that Jesus is God, or that God is one in three persons. This worried Rabaut, who said, "I will not reject a mystery for the only reason that it cannot be understood."

Rabaut knew no amount of freedom is worth the compromise of biblical teachings. "This freedom for which so many of our people yearn, I fear it as much as I desire it," he said. Still, he added, "I have no trouble putting my fate in the hands of Wise Providence."

Both of his observations have proven right. The church's freedom didn't last long. After the death of King Louis XVI, a group of violent revolutionaries gained power over the country and executed thousands of people whom they viewed as their political and religious enemies. Seeing religion as an enemy of progress, they imprisoned thousands of Roman Catholics, Jews, and Protestants, including Paul Rabaut, and killed many others, including one of Rabaut's sons. Churches were closed, religious monuments destroyed, and the word *saint* was removed from street names. A statue to Reason was erected in the cathedral to be worshiped as a goddess. Once again, pastors left the country or went into hiding. Still, in spite of this terrible time, known as the Reign of Terror, the church survived.

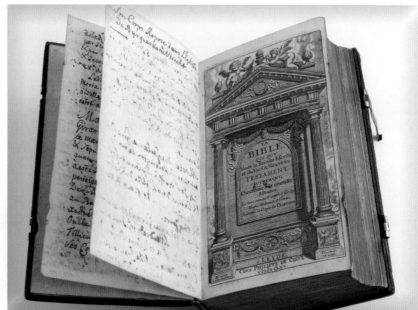

A Huguenot family Bible printed in 1665, with several pages of manuscript entries for the births and deaths of the children

Over the years, Marie's story has encouraged many believers to trust the same "God of mercy" who sustained her faith to the end. Especially in France, she has become a symbol of resistance and perseverance. Her letters have also helped historians understand how prisoners lived at the Tower of Constance and how Protestants helped each other during the persecution in France.

Marie never imagined her life would still be remembered three hundred years after her birth. Through both her long and terrible imprisonment and the poverty and disappointments she had to face when she returned home, she simply continued to do what God called her to do every day, keeping her eyes on the future "triumph of glory," loving those around her, and thanking God for what she described as "the honor of wearing His uniform for His just cause."

Time Line

1598–On April 13, Henry IV issues the Edict of Nantes for the toleration and protection of Protestants.

1685–Louis XIV revokes (puts an end to) the Edict of Nantes on October 18.

1700–Pierre Durand (Marie's brother) is born.

1702-1704–The War of the Camisards, in which Protestants rebelled in self-defense against the government, occurs. Some uprisings continue until 1710.

1711–Marie is born on July 15.

1715–On September 1, King Louis XIV dies. Antoine Court organizes a meeting of French Protestant pastors called a *synod*.

1719–Soldiers raid during a worship service. Claudine (Marie's mother) is arrested. Some guards stay at Marie's house for twenty-one days. Pierre escapes to Switzerland with a friend.

1724–A royal declaration demands the death of all Protestant preachers.

1726–First national synod (official meeting of church officers) since the Revocation of the Edict of Nantes. Pierre is ordained pastor.

1727–Pierre marries Anne Rouvier.

1729–Étienne is arrested and sent to Fort Brescou.

1730–Marie and Mathieu Serre are officially engaged on April 26.
    On July 14, Marie and Mathieu are arrested. Mathieu is sent to Fort Brescou and Marie to the Tower of Constance.

1731–Isabelle Rouvier, Pierre's mother-in-law, is imprisoned at the Tower on March 18.

1732–Pierre is captured and killed.

1738–Marie writes the first of her letters in the name of all the prisoners.

1743–Étienne is released from prison.

1747–Anne Rouvier Durand dies.

1749–Étienne dies.

1750–Mathieu Serre is released.

1752–The Marquis of Paulmy visits the Tower.

1754–Isabelle Rouvier dies.

1768–Marie is released.

1776–Marie dies.

1787–With the Edict of Toleration, Louis XVI allows his Protestant citizens some freedom (legalizes their baptisms and marriages).

1789–The French Revolution grants freedom of religion.

Pronunciation Key

This pronunciation key will give you an idea of how the French names in *Marie Durand* should be pronounced. For some of the sounds of the French language, though, there is not an exact English sound, so the best way to learn how to pronounce them is to hear them spoken in French. If you are able to use the Internet, you can hear these names pronounced correctly at https://www .howtopronounce.com/.

Antoine Court—AHN-twahn KOOR

Beauvau—bau-VOH

Bouchet—boo-SHAY

Brescou—bres-KOO

Claudine—kloh-DEEN

Durand—doo-RAHN

Étienne—eigh (as in eight)-tee-YEN

Isabeau Menet—ee-zah-BOH muh-NAY

Louis Phélypeaux de Saint-Florentin—loo-EE fay-lee-POH duh SEHN floh-ruhn-TEEN

Marie—mah-REE

Marie Vey-Goutète—mah-REE vay-goo-TEHT

Paulmy d'Argenson—paul-MEE dar-zhen-SON (This is a nasal sound, so the last syllable should sound like song, without the g on the end.)

Pierre—pee-AIR

Pranles—PRAHN-luh

Rabaut—RAH-boh

Rouvier—ROO-vee-ay

Did you know?

❀ People have often been amazed at the strong faith of the Protestant community where Marie lived, especially since it was mostly a rough and rugged population, living in a fairly isolated area. One of the reasons the gospel had spread so far into the country is that many people in remote areas traveled to the main cities to sell their products—mostly wheat, rye, clothes, or shoes. During those travels, they were able to hear Protestant preachers and buy Bibles and other books.

❀ About two hundred thousand Protestants left France after the 1685 Revocation of the Edict of Nantes. Many of them were merchants and craftsmen who ended up helping the economy of the countries where they moved. Some were scientists and writers. For example, Denis Papin, the first person to present to the Royal Society of London a design for a steamboat, was a French Protestant refugee who lived in England, Italy, and Germany.

Only two years after the Revocation, the Marquis de Vauban, the greatest military engineer in France at that time, asked the king to call back the Protestants. Besides talents and resources, France had lost many men who had been willing to fight for their country. Vauban repeated his request two years later, always without success. Later, many other people in France agreed that sending Protestants away had been a mistake.

❀ At the beginning of the eighteenth century, when Marie was born, the only forms of artificial light in Europe were still oil lamps, candles, and lanterns. Around that time, however, the larger cities in Europe started to use tall lanterns for street lighting. The lanterns were lit at night and turned off in the morning.

❀ As many houses in the area, Marie's house was built of stone. It was fairly big and had several rooms. Furniture was simple and made of wood. Poorer people had smaller houses with dirt floors and thatched roofs. In the winter, many farmers lived in their stables with sheep and goats and took advantage of the animals' body heat.

❀ During Marie's life, France was divided into three classes of people: the clergy (priests, bishops, cardinals, monks, and nuns); the nobles, or aristocrats (including judges, generals, and other influential and rich people who could buy the same benefits); and the common people. Some

of the common people, like the Durands and the Rouviers, had well-paying jobs (accountants, lawyers, doctors, merchants, and skilled craftsmen) and led better lives than others. This group later became known as the middle class. About 80 percent of the population of France, however, was made up of farmers or fishermen who often struggled to survive, especially when weather conditions or natural disasters caused a famine or when the government raised their taxes. Many people were forced to live on bread, chestnuts, and water and sell other products to pay taxes. Sometimes, even bread was scarce. This social injustice was a major cause of the French Revolution.

❀ The region where Marie lived was rich in chestnut trees. During the great freeze of 1709, when most of the crops died, chestnuts were the only product left. The chestnut tree was often nicknamed "bread tree." Chestnuts were roasted, boiled, or ground into flour. They could also be eaten raw or were dried and kept in storage for all-year-round use. When soaked overnight and boiled, chestnuts made a nourishing porridge (called *bajanat*) that was eaten with milk. Chestnut leaves were also picked to feed sheep and goats. The wood of the tree was used to build furniture or fences or to make beams to support houses. The small twigs were used to make baskets.

❧ Along with chestnuts, other common peasant foods were bread, porridges, vegetable soups, eggs, and cheese. Meat was eaten only on special occasions and was sometimes dried. Stale bread was used in soups. Most people had a cellar under the house, which always stayed cooler. There, they kept dry meats, oil, and cheese.

❧ Some of the gifts sent by supporters to the Tower of Constance included chestnuts (fresh and dry), lard, rice, butter, honey, olive oil, pepper, spices, lentils, and soap. The prisoners often sold the spices to their jailers and used the money to buy other needs.

❧ In spite of her young age, Marie's niece, Anne, also suffered from rheumatism. Knowing how painful the illness can be, Marie suggested she could travel to the town of Balaruc, on the French coast, which had been famous since ancient times for its natural hot springs. Because of their mineral contents, these waters were useful in the treatment of rheumatism. Marie also suggested mixing the hot springs water with sand and applying it to her painful joints. The hot springs resort at Balaruc is still there today.

❧ During the reign of Louis XIV (1643–1715, the longest reign in European history), France was strong and respected. It was the center of learning, gathering visitors from all over the world. By the end of the eighteenth century, French had become the main language of educated people. Many important American figures such as Washington, Jefferson, and Franklin spoke French as a second language.

❧ As other rulers in Europe, Louis XIV was an *absolute monarch*. That means he didn't have to respect the laws of the country. He was called the Sun King as a symbol of his great power. He believed he was reigning by divine right.

❧ Louis XIV had a huge appetite. His sister-in-law once wrote, "I have very often seen the king eat four plates of different soups, an entire pheasant, a partridge, a large plateful of salad, mutton cut up in its juice with garlic, two good pieces of ham, a plateful of cakes and fruits and jams."

Louis normally had his first meal at 10 a.m. As soon as he woke up, however, he drank a cup of bouillon or sage tea. He loved salads of raw and cooked vegetables dressed with oil, vinegar or lemon juice, salt, and spices and kept a large garden with produce for each season. Potatoes and tomatoes had just started coming from America, but they were not very common or popular.

The king's chefs also invented new sauces, such as *bèchamel*, or white sauce. Mayonnaise probably was invented in 1756. Coffee appeared in France under Louis XIV. Tea and cocoa were also popular drinks of kings and nobles. Being imported, they were still rare and expensive. Poor people drank water, milk, herbal teas, and especially homemade wine mixed with water.

Louis XIV made the town of Versailles, about fifteen miles west of Paris, the headquarters of his government. There, he transformed a palace that had been used as a hunting lodge into a huge and elaborate complex surrounded by astounding gardens, including many fountains with special effects. Every detail of the palace and its grounds was meant to glorify the king. He also made all the rich lords move to Versailles and threw many parties to keep them all entertained. At the same time, he was able to keep an eye on them. To impress them, he turned even his own daily life into a "reality show," and his courtiers could gather to watch him wake up, get dressed, eat meals, and prepare for bed. The kings that followed kept the same custom. Marie Antoinette, wife of King Louis XVI, complained, "I put on my rouge and wash my hands in front of the whole world."

❧ Many people remember Marie Antoinette as a clueless queen who, when she heard the peasants had no bread, said, "Let them eat cake." In reality, there is no proof she said this. The first person to use this quote was Jean Jacques Rousseau, one of the philosophers who lived at the time of Marie Durand. In his autobiography, written when Marie Antoinette was only nine and lived in Austria, he attributed this quote to "a great princess." And the French word was not cake, but *brioche*, which at that time was only a fine bread enriched with a little butter, sugar, and eggs.

❧ Six years before her release, Marie made a strong impression on a six-year-old boy who visited the Tower with his mother, a noblewoman who wanted to help the prisoners. Fifty-seven years after his visit, the boy, who had become an influential statesman, still remembered Marie vividly. He wrote, "I have seen this prisoner who remained there thirty-eight years…. She was a very pious person, full of reason and light, and greatly respected by the other prisoners, even if many were older than her."

A Letter from Marie to Her Niece, Anne

To Mr. Chiron, living at the Taconnerie,
To give, if it pleases him, to Mademoiselle Durand, in Geneva

The Tower of Constance
November 25, 1755

I should have answered your two letters as soon as I received them, two in the space of three days, my dear, but there has been some news about the freedom of some poor captives, and I wanted to make sure they were true before I wrote....

What gave us especially high hopes is that eight convicts were freed from their chains recently, and we were assured that we, miserable Maras,* would share in the same happiness. But it was a rumor.

Still, their freedom gives us great hope, especially when we hear that our free brothers invoke the holy name of God in numerous and frequent meetings, and nobody says a word. So, my dear angel, don't feel sad.

---

* Ruth 1:20: In the Bible, Naomi says her name is Mara, which means "bitter," because her husband and sons have died. Marie calls the women in the prison Maras, not because they are bitter but because they have lost much.

The times seem long, and, in fact, they are. Our flesh complains because we are naturally impatient, but, my dear girl, let's put to death our evil desires [Col. 3:5]. Let's be the violent who take heaven by force [Matt. 11:12]. Let's seek the kingdom of God and His righteousness, and all these things will be added unto us [Matt. 6:33]. Let's forsake our ways and return to the Lord who, in His greatest wrath, remembers mercy [Hab. 3:2]. He will have pity on His desolate Zion and will restore her to her renowned condition on the earth. Let's pray for her peace, for God has promised prosperity to those who love her [Ps. 122:6].

Ah, my dear little one, let's trust the Father of mercy, invoking Him with all the power we have in our souls, and He will have compassion on us. We will enjoy days of peace and serenity. We will still have the sweet satisfaction of seeing and embracing each other. Seeing a child whom I cherish and love more than myself would reach the height of my desires, and my happiness would be perfect in this world.

You are reading my letters through the eyes of your imagination, my little darling! It's the bond of friendship you have for me that hides all imperfections, because I am not paying much attention to style when I write to you. To tell you the truth, I never revise my letters, unless I write for adults. But, oh, what praise and commendations you send me! You make me blush! It's true that I am blessed to be loved and that no one hates me by the spirit of jealousy that often accompanies too many expressions of love, but this is not a merit of which I am worthy. It is the grace of God that wants to soften my bitterness.

In any case, my gentle little one, be always wise, sweet, patient, and moderate. Trust always in our divine Savior, and He will never forsake you.

You are ill, my dear child! I am so sorry! May the Lord, purely by His grace, give you the most robust health and send you soon into my arms! God will grant us this favor when we least expect it.

My health is pretty good, but I feel distressed because of you, and your sad state has much to do with it. If I could give you all the comfort you need, I would find again peace in my situation. But we must submit to the will of God and kiss the rod that strikes us....

Good-bye, my dear angel, good-bye, my everything. You may see me not as a good aunt, but as a tender mother. Always love me as I love you, and be sure that nothing but death will ever hinder my love for you.

Your sincere aunt,

La Durand

I am not sending you more shirts. I want to see how things progress because, if I am free, I will come to take you with me. My friend sends you sweet hugs. Please reply, my dear love, to the first letter you receive because I long to hear from you.

Acknowledgments

I am deeply grateful to all those who have generously shared their time, knowledge, and resources to make this book possible. I am first of all indebted to Francoise Anderson, who has inspired and fueled this idea even when I wondered if the story of a woman who spent thirty-eight years in prison, as inspiring as it was, could really fill sixty-four pages. It certainly did! In fact, I could have written much more. Francoise is writing a larger biography of Pierre and Marie Durand—quite possibly the first in the English language—so we were able to share our research and discuss questions and issues we encountered. She also provided me with a faithful translation of Marie's letters and reviewed my manuscript to ensure I had interpreted correctly—with my rusty knowledge of French—the information I had gathered from French sources.

I am also grateful to Dr. Otto Selles, professor of French studies at Calvin College, Grand Rapids, Michigan; Dr. Yves Krumenacker, French historian and professor of modern history at Jean Moulin University in Lyon, France; Dr. Lionel Laborie, visiting research fellow, Department of History, Goldsmiths University of London; and Dr. Martin Klauber, affiliate professor of church history at Trinity Evangelical Divinity School, Deerfield, Illinois, for their careful and patient review of my manuscript and their valuable insights. Gilles Despins, founder and teacher at ProFAC Theological School and avid student of the history of French Protestantism, has been of invaluable help in reading the manuscript and discussing with me some of the most puzzling events. He has also kindly provided most of the photos in this book.

As always, I thank my husband and children, my church family at Christ URC, and my friends for their continued support, particularly Timothy Massaro and Heather Chisholm-Chait, who read the manuscript and offered priceless advice. A special thanks to my Sunday school students Zoe and Evan Olow, Lucy Plotner, and James, Matthew, Adam, and Olivia Horton, who also read the manuscript (without pictures) and expressed their encouragement and valuable opinions.

Much of the credit is once again due to Dr. Joel Beeke, Jay Collier, Annette Gysen, Steve Renkema, David Woollin, and the rest of the staff at Reformation Heritage Books for their support, advice, encouragement, and unending patience, as well as to my exceptional illustrator, Matt Abraxas, who never ceases to amaze me. The quality and value of this book would be much less without the faithful contribution of these talented and committed individuals.